OLD
IS
THE
NEW
YOUNG

summersdale

OLD IS THE NEW YOUNG

Summersdale Publishers Ltd
46 West Street
Chichester
West Sussex
PO19 1RP
UK

www.summersdale.com

Printed and bound in the Czech Republic

ISBN: 978-1-84953-165-8

Substantial discounts on bulk quantities of Summersdale books are available to corporations, professional associations and other organisations. For details telephone Summersdale Publishers by telephone: +44 (0) 1243 771107, fax: +44 (0) 1243 786300 or email: nicky@summersdale.com.

OLD
IS
THE
NEW
YOUNG

Inside every older person
is a younger person –
wondering what the
hell happened.

Cora Harvey Armstrong

My wife said to me, 'I don't look fifty, do I darling?' I said 'Not any more.'

Bob Monkhouse

You only live once, but
if you do it right, once
is enough.

Mae West

Don't let ageing get you down. It's too hard to get back up.

John Wagner

Old age ain't no place
for sissies.

Bette Davis

Three things happen when you get to my age. First your memory starts to go... I've forgotten the other two.

Denis Healey

Seize the moment.
Remember all those women
on the *Titanic* who waved off
the dessert cart.

Erma Bombeck

I have the body of an
18-year-old. I keep it
in the fridge.

Spike Milligan

The older one grows, the
more one likes indecency.

Virginia Woolf

Beautiful young people are accidents of nature, but beautiful old people are works of art.

Eleanor Roosevelt

I'm not sixty,
I'm 'sexty'.

Dolly Parton

Eventually you will reach a point when you stop lying about your age and start bragging about it.

Will Rogers

You can't turn back the clock. But you can wind it up again.

Bonnie Prudden

It's sex, not youth,
that's wasted on
the young.

Janet Harris

We are young only once, after that we need some other excuse.

Anonymous

My doctor told me to do
something that puts me out
of breath, so I've taken up
smoking again.

Jo Brand

Men are like wine.
Some turn to vinegar,
but the best improve
with age.

C. E. M. Joad

The ageing process has you firmly in its grasp if you never get the urge to throw a snowball.

Doug Larson

When they tell me
I'm too old to do
something, I attempt
it immediately.

Pablo Picasso

The key to successful
ageing is to pay as little
attention to it as possible.

Judith Regan

The older you get the
more important it is
not to act your age.

Ashleigh Brilliant

As for me, except for an occasional heart attack, I feel as young as I ever did.

Robert Benchley

Old age is an excellent time for outrage. My goal is to… do at least one outrageous thing every week.

Maggie Kuhn

I don't want to retire.
I'm not that good at
crossword puzzles.

Norman Mailer

I'm aiming by the time
I'm 50 to stop being
an adolescent.

Wendy Cope

Men chase golf balls when
they're too old to chase
anything else.

Groucho Marx

First, you forget names...
Next, you forget to pull your
zipper up and finally you
forget to pull it down.

Leo Rosenberg

You can't help getting
older, but you don't
have to get old.

George Burns

I'd hate to die with a good liver... When I die I want everything to be knackered.

Hamish Imlach

I'm officially middle-aged.
I don't need drugs... I can
get the same effect just by
standing up real fast.

Jonathan Katz

I'm limitless as far as age is concerned... as long as he has a driver's licence.

Kim Cattrall on dating younger men

To get back my youth I would do anything in the world, except take exercise, get up early, or be respectable.

Oscar Wilde

You know you are
getting older when
'happy hour' is a nap.

Gary Kristofferson

Be kind to your kids, they'll
be choosing your
nursing home.

Anonymous

There is only one cure for grey hair. It was invented by a Frenchman. It is called the guillotine.

P. G. Wodehouse

Age is just a number. It's
totally irrelevant unless, of
course, you happen to be a
bottle of wine.

Joan Collins

I want to live to be 80
so I can piss more
people off.

Charles Bukowski

When people are old
enough to know better,
they're old enough to
do worse.

Hesketh Pearson

Passing the vodka bottle
and playing the guitar.

**Keith Richards on how
he keeps fit**

Few women admit
their age. Few men
act theirs.

Anonymous

If you obey all the
rules, you miss all
the fun.

Katharine Hepburn

I'll keep swivelling my hips
until they need replacing.

Tom Jones

I can still remember
when the air was
clean and the sex
was dirty.

George Burns

My grandmother's 90. She's dating. He's 93. They never argue. They can't hear each other.

Cathy Ladman

The older I get, the older old is.

Tom Baker

A man is only as old as the
woman he feels.

Groucho Marx

I don't plan to grow old
gracefully. I plan to have
facelifts until my ears meet.

Rita Rudner

Sex in the sixties is
great, but improves
if you pull over to the
side of the road.

Johnny Carson

We do not stop playing
because we grow old. We
grow old because we
stop playing!

Benjamin Franklin

Forty is the old age of
youth; fifty the youth
of old age.

Victor Hugo

The only form of
exercise I take
is massage.

Truman Capote

Time and trouble will tame
an advanced young woman,
but an advanced old woman
is uncontrollable by any
earthly force.

Dorothy L. Sayers

Not a shred of evidence
exists in favour of the idea
that life is serious.

Brendan Gill

I can still enjoy sex at 74. I live at 75, so it's no distance.

Bob Monkhouse

I'm too old to do things by half.

Lou Reed

As the talk turns to old age,
I say I am 49 plus VAT.

Lionel Blair

Laughter doesn't
require teeth.

Bill Newton

Do not worry about avoiding temptation. As you grow older it will avoid you.

Joey Adams

You can get away with
murder when you're 71
years old. People just think
I'm a silly old fool.

Bernard Manning

Is it not strange that desire should so many years outlive performance?

William Shakespeare,
Henry IV Part II

I can still cut the mustard...
I just need help opening
the jar!

Anonymous

Oh, to be 70 again.

Georges Clemenceau on seeing a
pretty girl on his 80th birthday

Doctors are always telling us that drinking shortens your life. Well I've seen more old drunkards than old doctors.

Edward Phillips

If I had my life to live over again, I'd make the same mistakes, only sooner.

Tallulah Bankhead

If you want a thing
done well, get a
couple of old broads
to do it.

Bette Davis

Interviewer: To what do you attribute your advanced age?

Malcolm Sargent: Well, I suppose I must attribute it to the fact that I have not died.

Old age is like a plane flying
through a storm. Once you
are aboard there is nothing
you can do.

Golda Meir

No man is ever old
enough to know
better.

Holbrook Jackson

One of the best parts of growing older? You can flirt all you like since you've become harmless.

Liz Smith

Another belief of mine:
that everyone else
my age is an adult,
whereas I am merely
in disguise.

Margaret Atwood

My grandmother
is over 80 and still
doesn't need glasses.
Drinks right out of
the bottle.

Henny Youngman

One should never make
one's debut in a scandal.
One should reserve that to
give interest to one's
old age.

Oscar Wilde

When I was young, I was told: 'You'll see when you're fifty.' I'm 50 and I haven't seen a thing.

Erik Satie

Life is too short to
learn German.

Richard Porson

Exercise daily. Eat wisely. Die anyway.

Anonymous

Old people should not eat
health foods. They need all
the preservatives they
can get.

Robert Orben

Interviewer: Can you remember any of your past lives?

The Dalai Lama: At my age I have a problem remembering what happened yesterday.

Middle age is when
it takes you all night
to do once what once
you used to do
all night.

Kenny Everett

Growing old is
compulsory, growing
up is optional.

Bob Monkhouse

My grandmother was a very tough woman. She buried three husbands and two of them were just napping.

Rita Rudner

As one grows older,
one becomes wiser
and more foolish.

François de La Rochefoucauld

There is no pleasure worth forgoing just for an extra three years in the geriatric ward.

John Mortimer

I smoke 10 to 15 cigars a day; at my age I have to hold on to something.

George Burns

When we're young we want
to change the world. When
we're old we want to change
the young.

Anonymous

Every morning, like clockwork, at 7 a.m., I pee. Unfortunately, I don't wake up till 8.

Harry Beckworth

I'm 78 but I still use a
condom when I have
sex. I can't take
the damp.

Alan Gregory

… long after wearing
bifocals and hearing aids,
we'll still be making love.
We just won't know
with whom.

Jack Paar

My nan said, 'What do you mean when you say the computer went down on you?'

Joseph Longthorne

An old man marrying
a young girl is like
buying a book for
someone else to read.

Jim Thompson

I wouldn't like to die on stage. I'd settle for room service and a couple of dissipated women.

Peter O'Toole

When I die I want to go like
my grandfather, peacefully
in his sleep. Not screaming,
like his passengers.

Anonymous

The older we get, the better we used to be.

John McEnroe

Bill Wyman couldn't be here tonight. He's at the hospital attending the birth of his next wife.

Frank Worthington

It's a sobering thought: when Mozart was my age, he had been dead for two years.

Tom Lehrer

The widower married his first wife's sister so he wouldn't have to break in a new mother-in-law.

Tony Hancock

Here's God's cruel joke: by the time a guy figures out how women work, his penis doesn't.

Adam Carolla

Old? He chases his
secretary around the desk
but can't remember why.

Leopold Fechtner

I'm in pretty good shape for the shape I'm in.

Mickey Rooney at 58

Middle age is when your age starts to show around your middle.

Bob Hope

Drinking removes
warts and wrinkles
from women I look at.

Jackie Gleason

When I die I want to be
cremated, and ten per cent
of my ashes thrown in my
agent's face.

W. C. Fields

Why have I lived so long? Jack Daniels and not taking shit from the press.

Frank Sinatra

My only regret in life is that I didn't drink more champagne.

John Maynard Keynes

I hope you die before me
because I don't want you
singing at my funeral.

Spike Milligan to Harry Secombe

Early to rise and early to
bed makes a man healthy,
wealthy and dead.

James Thurber

Do I exercise? Well I
once jogged to
the ashtray.

Will Self

I think all old folks' homes should have striptease. If I ran one I'd have a striptease every week.

Cynthia Payne

Are there sexy dead ones?

Sean Connery after being informed he was voted 'The Sexiest Man Alive' in a poll

I haven't had a hit film
since Joan Collins
was a virgin.

Burt Reynolds

Youth is when you're
allowed to stay up late on
New Year's Eve. Middle age
is when you're forced to.

Bill Vaughn

They say you shouldn't say nothing about the dead unless it's good. He's dead. Good.

Jackie Mabley

Always pat children on the head whenever you meet them, just in case they happen to be yours.

Augustus John

In dog years,
I'm dead.

Anonymous

True terror is to wake up
one morning and discover
that your high school class
is running the country.

Kurt Vonnegut

Red meat and gin.

Julia Child on the key to her longevity

Middle age is having
a choice between two
temptations and choosing
the one that'll get you
home earlier.

Dan Bennett

When grace is joined with
wrinkles, it is adorable.
There is an unspeakable
dawn in happy old age.

Victor Hugo

One man in his time
plays many parts.

William Shakespeare,
As You Like It

I'm not interested in age. People who tell me their age are silly. You're as old as you feel.

Elizabeth Arden

Middle age is when your old
classmates are so grey and
wrinkled and bald they don't
recognize you.

Bennett Cerf

All would live long, but none would be old.

Benjamin Franklin

Growing old is like being
increasingly penalised
for a crime you haven't
committed.

Anthony Powell

There will always be death and taxes; however, death doesn't get worse every year.

Anonymous

I refuse to admit that I
am more than 52, even if
that makes my children
illegitimate.

Nancy Astor

Pushing 40? She's
hanging on for
dear life.

Ivy Compton-Burnett

Regrets are the natural
property of grey hairs.

Charles Dickens

I don't have any children, I have four middle-aged people.

Dick Van Dyke

The years between 50 and
70 are the hardest. You are
always asked to do things,
and yet you are not decrepit
enough to turn them down.

T. S. Eliot

The past is the only
dead thing that
smells sweet.

Cyril Connolly

An archaeologist is the best husband a woman can have: the older she gets, the more interested he is in her.

Agatha Christie

Memorial services are the cocktail parties of the geriatric set.

Harold Macmillan

Youth is the time of getting,
middle age of improving,
and old age of spending.

Anne Bradstreet

The young sow wild oats,
the old grow sage.

Winston Churchill

You don't get older,
you get better.

Shirley Bassey

The long dull monotonous
years of middle-aged
prosperity or middle-aged
adversity are excellent
campaigning weather for
the Devil.

C. S. Lewis

Mrs Allonby: I delight in men over 70, they always offer one the devotion of a lifetime.

Oscar Wilde, *A Woman of No Importance*

My idea of hell is to be
young again.

Marge Piercy

Anyone can get old. All you
have to do is live
long enough.

Groucho Marx

I do wish I could tell you my age but it's impossible. It keeps changing all the time.

Greer Garson

He was either a man of 150
who was rather young for
his years, or a man of 110
who had been aged
by trouble.

P. G. Wodehouse, *Lord Emsworth
Acts for the Best*

I have wrestled with death.
It is the most unexciting
contest you can imagine.

Joseph Conrad

A man loves the meat
in his youth that he
cannot endure in
his age.

William Shakespeare, *Much Ado
About Nothing*

You know you're
getting old when the
candles cost more
than the cake.

Bob Hope

The young have aspirations
that never come to pass, the
old have reminiscences of
what never happened.

Saki

To me, old age is always 15
years older than I am.

Bernard Baruch

To stop ageing – keep on raging.

Michael Forbes

You're only young
once, but you can
always be immature.

Dave Barry

If you resolve to give up smoking, drinking and loving, you don't actually live longer. It just seems longer.

Clement Freud

The first sign of maturity
is the discovery that the
volume knob also turns to
the left.

Jerry M. Wright

You're never too old to become younger.

Mae West

Age seldom arrives
smoothly or quickly. It's
more often a succession
of jerks.

Jean Rhys

Old age isn't so bad
when you consider
the alternative.

Maurice Chevalier

KEEP CALM AND DRINK UP

£4.99

ISBN: 978-1-84953-102-3

Hardback

*'In victory, you deserve champagne;
in defeat, you need it.'*
Napoleon Bonaparte

BAD ADVICE FOR GOOD PEOPLE.

Keep Calm and Carry On, a World War Two government poster, struck a chord in recent difficult times when a stiff upper lip and optimistic energy were needed again. But in the long run it's a stiff drink and flowing spirits that keep us all going.

Here's a book packed with proverbs and quotations showing the wisdom to be found at the bottom of the glass.

ALL YOU NEED IS LOVE

£4.99

ISBN: 978-1-84953-130-6

Hardback

'Love is an irresistible desire to be irresistibly desired.'
Robert Frost

HEARTFELT WORDS FOR STARRY-EYED LOVERS.

When John Lennon wrote that 'all you need is love' back in 1967, perhaps he'd been struck by the lovebug himself. Love is a gift, love is an adventure, love is a many-splendoured thing – love is what makes the world go round, so why not spread a little of the sweet stuff right now?

Here's a book packed with quotations that will have you feeling the love in no time.

NOW PANIC AND FREAK OUT

£4.99

ISBN: 978-1-84953-103-0

Hardback

*'We experience moments absolutely free from worry.
These brief respites are called panic.'*
Cullen Hightower

BAD ADVICE FOR GOOD PEOPLE.

Keep Calm and Carry On is all very well, but life just isn't that simple. Let's own up and face facts: we're getting older, the politicians are not getting any wiser, and the world's going to hell in a handbasket.

It's time to panic.

Here's a book packed with quotations proving that keeping calm is simply not an option.

SHIT HAPPENS
SO GET OVER IT

£4.99

ISBN: 978-1-84953-132-0

Hardback

'Some days you're the bug.
Some days you're the windshield.'
Price Cobb

GOOD ADVICE FOR BAD TIMES.

So what if you've just wrapped your new car round a lamp post, emailed your 'personal' snaps to the entire company by mistake or delivered a eulogy with your flies undone: shit happens – get over it!

Here's a book packed with straight-talking quotations to help you get a grip and see the funny side.

www.summersdale.com